DO IT YOURSELF

KT-419-814

Saving Energy

Earth's Resources

Buffy Silverman

Heinemann LIBRARY

C153650368

www.heinemann.co.uk/library
Visit our website to find out more information about Heinemann Library books.

To order:
☎ Phone 44 (0) 1865 888066
📄 Send a fax to 44 (0) 1865 314091
💻 Visit the Heinemann bookshop at **www.heinemann.co.uk/library** to browse our catalogue and order online.

Heinemann Library is an imprint of **Pearson Education Limited**, a company incorporated in England and Wales having its registered office at Edinburgh Gate, Harlow, Essex, CM20 2JE – Registered company number: 00872828

Heinemann is a registered trademark of Pearson Education Limited.

Text © Pearson Education Limited 2008
First published in paperback in 2008
The moral rights of the proprietor have been asserted.

All rights reserved. No part of this publication may be reproduced in any form or by any means (including photocopying or storing it in any medium by electronic means and whether or not transiently or incidentally to some other use of this publication) without the written permission of the copyright owner, except in accordance with the provisions of the Copyright, Designs and Patents Act 1988 or under the terms of a licence issued by the Copyright Licensing Agency, Saffron House, 6–10 Kirby Street, London EC1N 8TS (www.cla.co.uk). Applications for the copyright owner's written permission should be addressed to the publisher.

Edited by Louise Galpine and Catherine Veitch
Designed by Richard Parker and Tinstar Design Ltd,
www.tinstar.co.uk
Illustrations Oxford designers and illustrators
Picture research by Hannah Taylor
Production: Victoria Fitzgerald

Originated by Chroma Graphics (Overseas) Pte. Ltd
Printed and bound in China by Leo Paper Group.

ISBN 978 0 431 111 24 7 (hardback)
12 11 10 09 08
10 9 8 7 6 5 4 3 2 1

ISBN 978 0 431 111 40 7 (paperback)
12 11 10 09 08
10 9 8 7 6 5 4 3 2 1

British Library Cataloguing in Publication Data
Silverman, Buffy
Saving energy : Earth's resources. - (Do it yourself)
333.7'916

A full catalogue record for this book is available from the British Library.

Acknowledegments
The publishers would like to thank the following for permission to reproduce photographs: ©Alamy pp. **25** (David R. Frazier Photolibrary, Inc.), **31** (Clynt Garnham), **33** (Trevor Smith), **41** (Jim West); ©Corbis pp. **5** (Royalty Free), **6** (epa/Rungroj Yongrit), **9** (Robert Garvey), **10** (epa/Jurnasyanto Sukarno), **24** (Reuters/Kimimasa Mayama), **27** (Royalty Free), **35** (Royalty Free), **42** (Michael DeYoung); ©Getty Images pp. **4** (Photodisc), **8** (Science Faction/Karen Kasmauski), **14** (Digital Vision), **23**, **37** (Sebun Photo/Satoru Imai), **38** (Stone/Charlie Waite), **39**; ©Photolibrary pp. **11** (Australian Only/Claver Carroll), **13** (Animals Animals/Robert Winslow), **17** (Index Stock Imagery), **29** (Australian Only/Ted Mead); ©Punchstock (Fancy) p. **15**; ©Science Photo Library pp. **7** (David Parker), **43** (Kevin A. Horgan).

Cover photograph of a compact fluorescent light bulb reproduced with permission of ©Corbis (Andrew Brookes).

Every effort has been made to contact copyright holders of any material reproduced in this book. Any omissions will be rectified in subsequent printings if notice is given to the publishers.

The publishers would like to thank Nicholas Lapthorn for his help in the preparation of this book.

Disclaimer
All the Internet addresses (URLs) given in this book were valid at the time of going to press. However, due to the dynamic nature of the Internet, some addresses may have changed, or sites may have changed or ceased to exist since publication. While the author and publishers regret any inconvenience this may cause readers, no responsibility for any such changes can be accepted by either the author or the publishers. It is recommended that adults supervise children on the Internet.

**KENT
LIBRARIES & ARCHIVES**
C153650368

Contents

Any words appearing in the text in bold, **like this**, are explained in the glossary.

What is energy?

You enter your room and switch on the lights. You sit at your desk and turn on a computer, sending messages to your friends. Feeling thirsty, you go to the refrigerator and get a cold drink.

Lights, computers, and refrigerators all do work for people. We depend on them and the **electricity** that runs them. Electricity is a type of **energy**.

We depend on other sources of energy, too. People fill up their cars with fuel so they can drive them. Miners dig coal from deep in the Earth. Coal is burned to make heat and electricity. We use **natural gas** for cooking and heat. Some people burn wood to cook and stay warm.

Electricity is needed to power computers and lights.

Energy to live and grow

Your body needs energy, too. Where does your energy come from? Your body runs on the energy in the food you eat. All living things need energy to live and grow.

Green plants absorb the Sun's energy to make food in their leaves. Some animals eat plants and depend on that food for energy. Other animals eat animals that eat those plants. All our food energy comes from the Sun, through plants and animals.

Types of energy

Energy is defined as the ability to do work. Energy can make an object move. The energy in wind moves a leaf. The energy in a stream turns a water wheel. A person uses energy when he or she lifts something. Work can also mean warming or lighting something.

Pick up a rock and balance it at the edge of a picnic table. The rock has **potential energy**. It is not doing work now, but it is in a position where it can do work. If you bump the table, the rock falls. The falling rock has moving energy, called **kinetic energy**. You can use your body's energy to pick the rock up again and place it on the table. That gives the rock more potential energy.

We depend on energy when we travel, work, and play.

Fossil fuels

Petrol is made from oil that has been taken from the ground. The oil we use today formed more than 300 million years ago.

Oil, coal, and **natural gas** are **fossil fuels**. Fossil fuels formed from the **fossil** remains of dead plants and animals. It took hundreds of millions of years for heat and pressure inside the Earth to turn fossils into fuel. When fossil fuels are burned, they give off **energy** that was once part of the plants and animals that formed them.

The energy in fossil fuels originally came from the Sun. Plants used the Sun's energy to make food, and animals ate the plants. When these plants and animals died, energy was trapped in their bodies. That energy is now in fossil fuels.

Using energy

Energy cannot be created or destroyed, but it can change from one form to another. When a car's engine burns petrol, chemical energy in fuel changes into heat energy. Hot air pushes pistons in a car engine, turning heat energy into motion energy.

A car engine burns petrol to move.

Under the ocean

Tiny floating **algae** called **diatoms** are thought to be the source of oil. Diatoms live in oceans. Like plants, they use the Sun's energy to make food, and they are eaten by many animals.

Millions of years ago, diatoms sunk to the bottom of the ocean after they died. Mud and rocks covered them. With little oxygen beneath the mud and rocks, they did not **decompose**. Pressure from rocks and heat from the earth gradually turned diatoms into oil. Eventually ancient seas shifted, and pockets of oil were left beneath layers of sand, silt, and rocks.

Oil rigs pump oil from underground.

Today, oil is found by drilling deep into the Earth. Oil collects in tiny droplets in open spaces in rocks. Huge oil rigs pump oil from below ground. It travels through pipelines or by ships to refineries around the world. At a refinery, thick black oil is heated and made into petrol, jet fuel, liquid gas, kerosene, and other products.

Mining coal and natural gas

People first began mining coal in China 3,000 years ago. They used it to **smelt** copper. In the 1700s people used coal to power steam engines in factories. Goods were sent around the world on coal-powered ships and trains. Although coal is no longer commonly used to power steam engines, it is still burned to make steel and other materials. Today, 40 per cent of the world's **electricity** is made by burning coal.

If coal is near the Earth's surface, it is dug up in strips in a process known as strip mining.

Swampy earth

Where does coal come from? Like oil, it is a fossil fuel. Three hundred million years ago, before dinosaurs lived on the Earth, the land was covered with swamps. Towering ferns, trees, and other plants grew. When trees and ferns died, they sank to the bottom of these swamps. They formed a spongy mass called **peat**. Layers of sand and clay covered the peat. The sand and clay gradually turned to rock. Over millions of years, the pressure from rocks turned peat into coal. When we burn coal today, we use the energy from those ancient ferns and trees.

Gas beneath the Earth

Natural gas is another fossil fuel. We use it for cooking and to heat water and homes. It can also be used to make electricity. Factories around the world use natural gas to make different goods. After oil and coal, natural gas is the energy source most used in Great Britain and the United States.

Like coal and oil, natural gas is made from the remains of plants and animals that lived millions of years ago. When tiny ocean plants and animals died, they sank to the bottom of the ocean. They were buried, along with sand and silt. Over many years the layers of sand and silt became thousands of feet thick. The plants and animals eventually became fossils. Heat and pressure gradually changed the fossils into gas, which was trapped in the layers of rock.

A well is drilled to **extract** natural gas from deep in the Earth.

Climate change

Fossil fuels are **non-renewable resources**. They take millions of years to form and cannot be replaced when they are gone. No one knows for sure how much fossil fuel we have left in the Earth. Scientists estimate that if people continue to use fossil fuels as they do today, there will be enough oil for about 45 years, gas for about 72 years, and coal for about 252 years.

The changing planet

For the last 250 years, people have increasingly used fossil fuels. When fossil fuels burn, they give off a gas called **carbon dioxide**. Carbon dioxide goes into the **atmosphere**. Scientists think that there is now more carbon dioxide in the atmosphere than there has been at any time in the past 20 million years.

Floods along coastal areas may become more common as the Earth's temperature warms.

Carbon dioxide and other gases in the atmosphere trap the Sun's heat and warm the planet. Without these gases, the Earth would not be warm enough for plants or animals to live on it. But too much carbon dioxide means that more of the Sun's heat is trapped in the atmosphere. As a result, the Earth's climate is changing. It is getting warmer.

As the temperature rises on Earth, scientists think that sea levels will rise, too. That means that some coastal cities will be flooded. People will no longer be able to live in some coastal communities. There may be more hurricanes, droughts, and other extreme weather. Glaciers will melt. Farmers may not be able to grow crops in certain areas. Other places may have a longer growing season. Some plants and animals will become **extinct**.

Climate change can cause droughts, making it hard for farmers to grow food.

Warming up

During the past 100 years, the average air temperature on Earth has increased by about 0.74° C (1.33° F). Scientists expect the air temperature to continue to get warmer. By burning less fossil fuel, however, people may be able to slow down climate change.

How does global warming work?

For this activity you will need:
* One large plastic plastic bottle
* Two glass jars of the same size
* Two thermometers
* Scissors
* A notebook

1 Soak the bottle in warm water and remove the label.

2 Carefully cut off the bottom third of the plastic bottle, leaving the top section and the lid. Make sure the top section is large enough to cover a jar. You can ask an adult for help cutting the bottle.

3 Put a thermometer inside each jar. Place both jars in a sunny spot, without covering them. Record the temperature.

4 Put the plastic bottle over one jar. Leave the other jar uncovered.

5 Record the temperature of each jar after one hour.

Heat trap

Which of your jars had the warmer temperature? Why do you think the air inside the covered jar was warmer than the air in the uncovered jar?

The plastic bottle in your experiment acted like a greenhouse. The Sun's **energy** warmed the air in both jars. The warm air in the covered jar could not escape and mix with the surrounding air. The warm air was trapped inside the plastic bottle. Just as the plastic bottle trapped heat, gases in the Earth's atmosphere trap heat and warm the air.

Fossil fuels are burned in factories to make machines run. When fossil fuels are burned, **pollutants** go into the air.

Carbon dioxide is one of the gases in the atmosphere that absorbs the Sun's energy. **Methane** is another of these gases. Because these gases absorb the Sun's energy, it does not escape into outer space. It warms the land and sea and makes the Earth warm enough for living things. This is called the **greenhouse effect**.

Burning oil, coal, and **natural gas** releases carbon dioxide into the atmosphere. That means there are more greenhouse gases to trap more of the Sun's energy. The air that surrounds us gets warmer. Most of the extra greenhouse gases in the atmosphere are from burning fossil fuels.

Energy conservation

Most of the **energy** people use comes from non-renewable **fossil fuels**. Cars and buses run on petrol. The energy for cooking and heating homes comes from **natural gas**. Coal is burned to make **electricity**. These fuels took millions of years to form.

The supplies of fossil fuels on Earth are limited. We cannot make more of them in a short time. If people keep using fossil fuels as we do today, there will not be enough oil, natural gas, or coal in the future.

One way to make fossil fuels last for a longer time is to **conserve** energy. Conserving energy means using less energy and reducing waste. By burning less fossil fuel, the air is cleaner. We add less **carbon dioxide** to the **atmosphere**, so there is less global warming.

Train passengers use less energy than if each person drove a car.

Energy efficiency

Your body uses food as fuel. You use the energy in food when you think, run, sleep, and breathe. But your body does not turn all of the energy in food into energy it can use. Most of the energy is lost as heat. When you exercise, you get warm. You can feel the heat that your body loses.

The machines we use also lose part of the energy that powers them. Switch on a lamp, and the energy in electricity is changed into light energy. But some of the energy is turned to heat. A light bulb feels hot because the bulb loses energy as heat. **Energy efficiency** is a measure of how much useful work a machine gets from fuel. An energy-efficient light bulb makes less heat and more light than an **incandescent light bulb**.

One way to conserve energy is to buy more energy-efficient products. Some cars use less fuel. There are refrigerators and washing machines that run on less electricity. An energy-efficient boiler uses less natural gas. Let's look at more ways to conserve energy.

Switch off a light and you conserve energy.

1 Fill a glass with water that is about room temperature. Using the thermometer, measure and record the water temperature.

2 Put the glass of water in the refrigerator. Measure and record the temperature every 5 minutes for 15 minutes. Calculate how much the temperature changes.

3 Refill the glass with room temperature water. Measure and record the water temperature again.

4 Put the glass in the cardboard box. Fill the space between the glass and box with foam pellets. Close the lid of the box.

5 Place the box with the glass in the refrigerator. Measure the temperature every 5 minutes for 15 minutes. Does the temperature change at a different rate?

Trapping warm air in

For this activity you will need:

* A thermometer
* A glass of water
* A small cardboard box with a lid. (The box should be slightly bigger than the glass.)
* Foam packing pellets
* A clock
* A notebook to record data

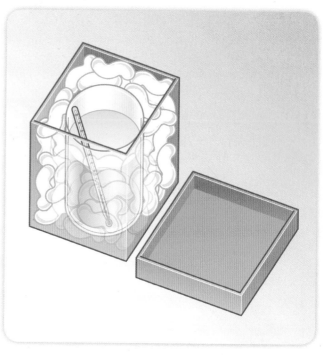

Insulation in the roof and walls of a house keeps warm air from flowing outside in winter. In the summer, an insulated home stays cooler.

Hold that warmth!

When you placed the glass of water in the refrigerator, the water cooled and the temperature went down. Heat energy moves to cooler areas. Heat energy moved from the warm water to the cooler surrounding air. The second glass, insulated by a box with foam pellets, cooled at a slower rate. The **insulation** slowed the movement of warmth to the surrounding cold air.

Insulation in a home works in a similar way. The walls and windows of many homes have insulation. It takes less energy to heat and cool an insulated home. In winter, insulation slows down the movement of warm inside air to the cold outside. In summer, insulation slows the movement of cool air to the hot outside.

Hot or cold?

Turning down the thermostat by 1 °C (34 °F) can cut 10 per cent from your home's energy bill.

Ways to save

Steps to follow

Testing insulation

For this activity you will need:

* Two thermometers
* A chair
* Masking tape

1 Test your home's **insulation** on a cold, windy day. Tape one thermometer to a chair and put the chair in the middle of a room.

2 Tape the other thermometer to an outside wall of the room, at the same height.

3 Record the temperature of the air in the middle of the room and on the outside wall.

4 Compare the temperatures every hour for four hours.

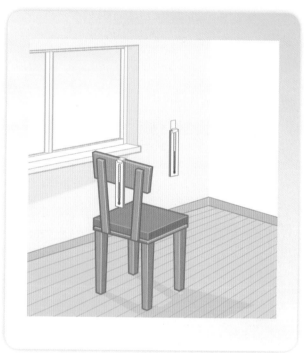

What is happening?

If you found little difference in the temperatures of the outside wall and the middle of the room, your wall has a lot of insulation. A larger difference means there is less insulation. Test several walls in your home.

Heat is lost through windows and walls of a home. Insulation slows airflow, so less **energy** is needed for heating or cooling.

Steps to follow

1 Warm air can escape around doors and windows. Make a draught detector to find where air flows out. Tear off a piece of plastic wrap, about 13 by 26 cm (5 by 10 inches).

2 Tape the short side of the plastic wrap to a pencil.

3 Hold up your detector and blow on it. Flowing air makes the plastic move.

4 On a windy day check for draughts. A draught shows that air is moving out of your house. Hold the detector about 2.5 cm (1 inch) from where the window glass meets the window frame. Watch to see if the plastic moves.

5 Check for draughts along door frames, light fixtures, and fans. Record where you find draughts.

How to find draughts

For this activity you will need:
* A pencil
* Sticky tape
* A piece of clear plastic wrap

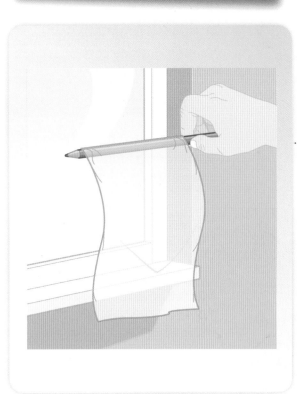

Fixing a draught

A draught shows where warm air flows to the outside. Show an adult where you found draughts. He or she can seal draughty doors and window edges and any other gaps.

Steps to follow

Making a draught excluder

For this activity you will need:

* Fabric, about 15 by 96 cm (6 by 38 inches)

* 1 kg (2 pounds) of dry rice or lentils

* A funnel or a jug with a spout

* A sewing machine or needle and thread

* Scissors

* Optional: Glue, wiggly eyes and fabric scraps for decoration.

1 Cut a piece of fabric, about 15 by 96 cm (6 by 38 inches).

2 Ask an adult to help you sew it. Fold the fabric lengthwise, so the right side of the material is on the inside. Stitch along one short and one long side.

3 Turn the fabric right side out. It will form a long tube that is open at one end.

4 Using the funnel, carefully pour rice or lentils into the tube.

5 Stitch the opening closed.

6 Optional: Add eyes and a tongue to make your draught excluder look like a snake.

7 Place your draught excluder along the bottom of a draughty door. Test your draught excluder. Does it block flowing air?

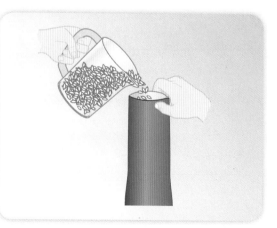

Warning: Ask an adult to help you with this activity.

What next?

Make draught exluders to put along draughty doors. Sew an extra one and give it as a gift to a friend or relative.

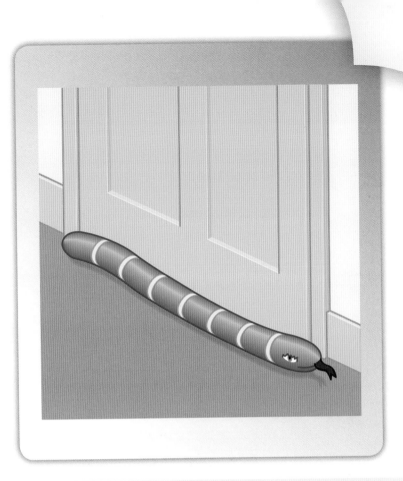

Energy-saving tips

Turn it off!

When you have finished using something, turn it off. A television that is turned off but plugged in is on standby and still uses some **electricity**. Unplug electronic equipment when it is not being used. Always turn off lights when you have finished using them.

Wear a jumper!

Instead of turning up the heat, put on a jumper. Keep the thermostat at the lowest comfortable setting. At night, use an extra blanket and turn the heat down a little more. Close your curtains on cold days to keep warm air in.

Take a shower!

Heating water uses about 15 per cent of a family's energy bill. Take a shower instead of a bath to save hot water. Use a kitchen timer to make sure your shower is five minutes or less.

Steps to follow

1 Ask an adult to put an energy-efficient light bulb (CFL) in a lamp.

2 Turn the lamp on for five minutes. Hold a thermometer 15 cm (6 inches) above the bulb for one minute. Measure and record the temperature.

3 Wait for the bulb to cool down. Ask an adult to take out the CFL and place an incandescent bulb in the same lamp.

4 Turn the lamp on for five minutes. Hold a thermometer 15 cm (6 inches) above the bulb for one minute. Measure and record the temperature.

A bright idea

For this activity you will need:

* One **incandescent light bulb** rated with the same light level as an energy-efficient bulb (CFL). (A 60-W incandescent bulb is equivalent to a 13-18-W CFL bulb. A 100-W incandescent bulb is equivalent to a 20-25-W CFL bulb.)
* A lamp
* A thermometer

Warning: Adult supervision is required for this project.

Make a difference

Saving energy at home is a great way to reduce greenhouse gases. Energy use in the average home creates about twice as much carbon dioxide as energy used by the average car.

More light, less heat

Which bulb produced more heat? You probably found the incandescent bulb created more heat. An incandescent bulb turns about 10 per cent of its energy into light and 90 per cent into heat. Energy-efficient bulbs (also called **compact fluorescent**, or CFL bulbs) use one-third the energy of an incandescent bulb to produce the same amount of light. That's because less energy is wasted as heat. They also produce 70 per cent less heat than an incandescent bulb.

One of the easiest ways to save energy in your home is to use energy-efficient light bulbs. Since most electricity is made with **fossil fuels**, you also put less **carbon dioxide** in the **atmosphere** when you use them. Share what you have learned about energy-efficient bulbs.

Energy-efficient bulbs cost more to buy than incandescent bulbs, but they last about 10–12 times longer. So overall, it is cheaper to use energy-efficient bulbs.

Fuels for the future

Conserving energy helps make **fossil fuels** last for a longer time and reduces greenhouse gases. But people will still need more energy in the future. More and more people in the world are demanding more and more energy. How will we have **electricity** in the future if fossil fuels are used up? How can we use energy without causing global warming?

Renewable energy resources

Renewable energy resources can help solve our energy needs for today and in the future. Unlike fossil fuels, renewable energy resources can be replenished in a short time, so we will not run out of them.

Solar panels on this solar car turn sunlight into electricity that powers the car.

Solar collectors on a roof heat water for a home.

Solar energy is one kind of renewable energy. Power from the Sun can be turned into heat and electricity. Wind is another renewable energy resource that has been used for hundreds of years to grind grain, pump water, and help farmers get water to crops. Modern windmills create electricity. Water has also been used in the past for powering machines. Today, river water drives **turbines** to make electricity. The oceans' tides can also turn turbines and make electricity. Fuels made from corn, sugarcane, grasses, and leftover frying oil can power cars and buses. Even rubbish is used for energy. All of these renewable energy resources are being used today, although they do not yet provide a large share of our energy.

We will never run out of power from the Sun, wind, and water. As people learn to harness and store the energy from these resources, more and more of our power will come from them. Unlike fossil fuels, energy from solar, wind, and water does not add greenhouse gases to the **atmosphere**, so they do not cause global warming.

Steps to follow

Solar collectors

For this activity you will need:

* Two disposable pie plates: one large, one small
* Black paint (non-water soluble)
* A paintbrush
* A measuring jug
* Water
* Two thermometers
* Plastic wrap
* Old clothes

1 Wearing old clothes, paint the inside bottom of the pie plates black and let them dry.

2 Bring your supplies to a sunny spot.

3 Measure and pour 250 ml (1 cup) of water into each pie plate.

4 Place a thermometer in each plate. Cover the pie plates with plastic wrap.

5 Measure and record the initial temperature of each pie plate.

6 Measure and record the temperature after 5, 10, and 15 minutes.

The Sun warms water

You probably found that the water temperature in both plates rose. The black paint absorbs the Sun's heat and warms the water. By concentrating the Sun's rays, the pie plates act as solar collectors. Which plate has warmer water? With a larger solar collector, more heat is absorbed, and the temperature increases more. A larger solar collector can do more work because it absorbs more heat. A solar water heating system works in the same way.

Some power stations concentrate solar power by using hundreds of curved mirrors. The mirrors focus sunlight on a pipe containing oil. Sunlight heats the oil. The oil is so hot that it boils water and makes steam. The steam turns a turbine to generate electricity.

Solar energy

Water for a building can be heated using the Sun. A flat box is placed on a roof. Inside the flat box are small tubes containing fluid. The tubes are attached to a plate that is painted black. The Sun heats up the black plate. The hot plate warms fluid flowing in the tubes. The tubes connect to a storage tank that holds the hot water.

Solar energy can also make electricity. The sunlight falling on the United States in one day has more than twice the energy used there in a year. But a lot of land is needed to harness enough energy to make electricity.

Steps to follow

A solar oven

For this activity you will need:

* A pizza box
* Newspaper
* Black paper
* Clear plastic wrap
* Aluminium foil
* Scissors
* Double-sided sticky tape
* A ruler
* A marker pen
* A thermometer

 1 Tape black paper to the inside, bottom surface of a pizza box.

 2 On the cover of the box, draw a large square, 2.5 cm (1 inch) from all edges.

 3 With scissors, carefully cut along three sides, leaving the fourth side as a hinge.

 4 Lift the flap, bending it at the hinge. Cover the inside of the flap with foil and tape it in place.

 5 Roll up a newspaper, so it forms a tube about 3.5 cm (1.5 inches) thick. Line the inside edges of the pizza box with four newspaper rolls. The newspaper will insulate your oven, keeping heat inside.

 6 Stretch plastic wrap over the opening, on the inside of the box. Tape the plastic along all four sides.

7 Prop open the lid with a ruler and position the pizza box so the foil reflects Sun into the oven.

 8 After your oven has heated for 15 minutes, place a thermometer inside and measure the temperature. How much warmer is your oven than the surrounding air?

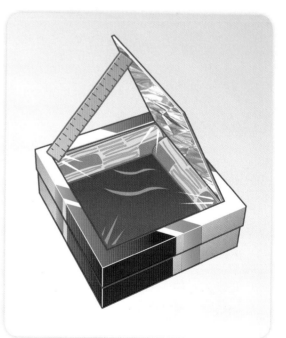

How does it work?

Sunlight reflects off the aluminium foil and is directed inside the oven. The black surface of the box absorbs the Sun's heat. The plastic wrap holds in heat, but allows light to shine through. Newspaper insulates the box to keep heat from escaping.

Photovoltaic cells on this roof turn the Sun's energy into electricity for this building.

Electricity from the Sun

You might have machines in your home that use solar power. Many calculators and watches have **photovoltaic cells** that turn the Sun's energy into electricity. Photovoltaic cells also power space satellites. They can provide electricity to pump water in a farmer's fields, or to provide power for a house.

Wind and water power

Steps to follow

1 An **anemometer** measures wind speed. You can make an anemometer to measure wind speed near your home. Start by colouring the outside of a paper cup with a brightly coloured marker.

2 With a pencil, draw two lines across a paper plate so that the lines meet at the centre of the plate.

3 Place a piece of tape on each cup. Stick the cups to the edge of the plate. Make sure all the cups face the same direction.

4 Push the pin through the centre of the plate. Stick the pin into the eraser-end of the pencil.

5 Take your anemometer outside on a windy day. Hold it up in the wind so it spins.

6 Count the number of times that you see the marked cup go around in one minute. That is the wind speed in revolutions per minute. Record the wind speed, noting the date and time.

Making an anemometer

For this activity you will need:

* A paper plate
* Four paper cups (all the same size)
* A marker pen
* A ruler
* A drawing pin
* A pencil with eraser
* Double-sided tape
* A watch with a second hand
* A notebook for recording your observations

7 For the next few days, measure the wind speed at different times of the day. Record the wind speed in different areas near your home. Where is the windiest place near your home? Where would you put a wind **turbine**?

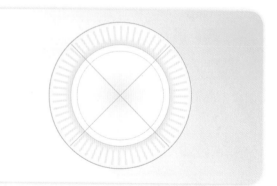

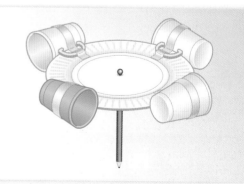

Using wind power

Today, wind turbines turn the **energy** from moving air into **electricity**. For a turbine to work, it must be located in a windy place. The amount of electricity made depends on the size of the turbines and the speed of the wind.

An important option

Wind power generates about 1 per cent of the world's electricity and is one of the fastest-growing forms of alternative energy. More than 20 per cent of Denmark's electricity comes from wind power.

Wind farms with hundreds of turbines are sited on land or offshore, where steady winds blow.

Making a wind turbine

For this activity you will need:

* One square piece of paper, 21 by 21 cm (8.5 by 8.5 inches)
* A drawing pin
* A pencil with eraser
* Scissors
* A ruler

 1 Draw two diagonal lines from one corner of the square paper to the opposite corner. The lines should cross in the centre of the paper.

 2 Using the drawing pin, punch a small hole where the lines meet.

 3 Mark each line 2.5 cm (1 inch) from the centre. Cut along the lines from the corners, stopping at the marks.

 4 Make a small hole with the drawing pin in the upper left corner of each flap.

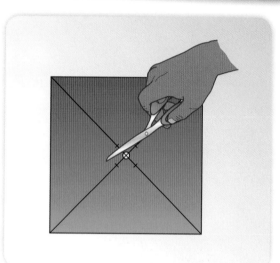

 5 Curl up the corner holes, lining them up over the centre hole.

6 Push the pin through all five holes and into the side of the eraser. Be sure that it is not fastened too tightly, so it can spin.

 7 Take your wind turbine outside and watch the wind make it spin.

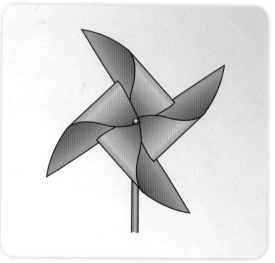

Capturing the wind

Most wind turbines are on towers 30 metres (100 feet) or more above ground. Because they are high above the ground, they capture the most wind. The largest wind turbines in the world are in the Scottish North Sea. They have three blades that form a circle 126 metres (413 feet) wide. If the blades were spread out, they would be the length of two football fields.

A wind turbine has two or three blades. The blades are designed to spin like a propeller. The blades connect to a shaft that spins when the blades turn. The turning shaft spins a **generator** that makes electricity.

Some farms and houses have a single wind turbine to provide electricity. At a wind farm, dozens of huge turbines generate enough electricity for many homes. Wind farms are often built in flat, open areas where the wind blows 22.5 kilometres (14 miles) per hour or more.

Wind turbines on this school playground generate electricity. The turbines produce more electricity per year than the school uses. Extra electricity is sold to the local power company and used by neighbouring homes.

Energy from water

For this activity you will need:

* A large cardboard milk or juice carton, washed
* A nail or drawing pin
* Masking tape
* A marker pen
* A ruler
* A notebook for recording data

 1 Carefully cut off the top of the carton.

 2 Measuring from the bottom of the carton, mark a dot in the centre of one panel at 2.5 cm (1 inch), 5 cm (2 inches), and 7.5 cm (3 inches). Using a nail or dawing pin, punch a hole in each mark.

 3 Cover the holes with one long piece of masking tape down the length of the carton.

 4 Mark a line 5 cm (2 inches) from the top of the carton.

 5 Bring your carton to a sink and fill it to the line. Put the carton on the edge of the sink, with the holes facing the sink.

 6 Pull off the tape. Watch how the water streams out. From which hole did the water stream the furthest? How did the water stream change as the water drained from the carton? Record your findings.

 7 Retape all holes, each with a single piece of tape. Refill the carton to the line.

 8 Remove the bottom tape. Measure the distance that the water flows, from the bottom edge of the carton to the point where it landed in the sink.

 9 Retape the holes. Refill the carton to the line. Remove the top tape. Measure the distance that the water flows.

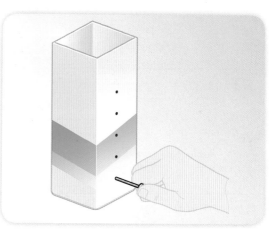

What is happening?

The water above an opening in the carton pushed down on the water below it. Water flowed farthest from the lowest hole because it had more water pushing down on it. Water has more energy when it is pushed by water above it.

Harnessing water power

Hydroelectric plants are built at the bottom of a dam. Water is funnelled from the dam through a tunnel. The force of the falling water turns a turbine's blades, making the turbine spin. The turbine spins a generator that produces electricity.

Rushing water spins turbines at a hydroelectric power station, and makes electricity.

Steps to follow

Water power

For this activity you will need:

* A ruler
* Newspaper
* A drinking straw
* Food colouring (optional)
* 240 ml (1 cup) of water
* A notebook for recording data

1 Do this activity outdoors and wear old clothes, because food colouring can stain your clothing.

2 Add a couple of drops of food colouring to water. The food colouring will make your results easier to see.

3 Spread newspaper on a pavement, or other smooth surface.

4 Put the drinking straw in the cup of water and cover the top of the straw with your finger. Hold the straw vertically, with the bottom of it about 30 cm (12 inches) above the ground. Release the water by lifting your finger from the straw.

5 Measure how far the water splashed from where it hit the ground. Record the size of the splash and the height at which you released the water.

6 What will happen if you double the height at which you release the water? Release another straw full of water from a height of 60 cm (24 inches). Measure how far the water splashes when it hits the ground and record your data.

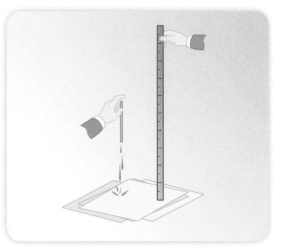

Falling water

A hydroelectric power plant gets energy from falling water. Does the height that water falls affect the amount of energy it produces? You probably found that releasing water from a greater height produced a larger splash. When water falls from a greater height, it has more energy.

At a hydroelectric plant, a dam raises the level of the water. The water behind the dam has more **potential energy**, because it has further to fall. When the water is released, it has more energy to spin a turbine and produce electricity. The amount of water that falls, and the distance it falls, determines the energy that falling water contains to make electricity.

A large **reservoir** of water forms behind a dam at a hydroelectric power station. Water is released through a tunnel under the dam and directed over a turbine. The spinning turbine generates electricity.

Using energy from plants and animals

People have always relied on plants for **energy**. Plants use the Sun's energy to make their food. When we eat plants, we take in that energy. Today, people also grow crops to make fuel and **electricity** as well as for eating. **Biomass** fuels are made from plants such as corn, soybeans, or sugarcane. The plants are **fermented** to make a liquid fuel called **ethanol**. Ethanol is usually blended with petrol and is used as a fuel for cars and lorries. By using ethanol combined with petrol, cars burn fewer **fossil fuels**.

Ethanol made from corn and other plants is combined with petrol.

Scientists are experimenting with new ways to make ethanol. They are trying to make ethanol from the woody fibres in trees, grasses, and crop wastes. Fast-growing trees and grasses would not need **fertilizers** that are made from fossil fuels. Making ethanol from crop wastes like corn stalks would **recycle** material that is now thrown away.

Growing fuel

Brazil is the world's largest producer of ethanol. Many cars in Brazil run on ethanol made from sugarcane.

Fuel from chips

Can old chip-frying oil run a bus? Yes! **Biodiesel** fuels can be made from waste oil from restaurants. Instead of throwing away cooking oil that was used to fry fish, chips, and other foods, it is recycled and turned into a fuel. Buses and lorries with diesel engines can run on this fuel. Biodiesel is also made from crops such as soybeans and rapeseed. It makes less air pollution than diesel fuel made from oil.

Do biomass fuels contribute to global warming? Burning these fuels does add **carbon dioxide** to the **atmosphere**. But when plants make food, they use carbon dioxide. The plants that biomass fuels are made of absorb carbon dioxide from the atmosphere as they grow.

This lorry delivers used vegetable oil from restaurants to a plant that will convert the oil into fuel.

Steps to follow

1 Pour water over 10 beans and soak them overnight in a bowl.

2 The next morning, drain the water from the beans.

3 Put the beans in a zip-top bag. Squeeze the air out of the bag and zip it closed.

4 Place the bag in a dark place such as a cupboard.

5 Check the bag once a day for two weeks and record your observations.

6 Do the rotting beans produce gas? Look for small gas bubbles on individual beans. The bag might also become inflated with gas around the beans. Do not open the bag while you are observing it.

Energy from food waste

For this activity you will need:

* A zip-top plastic bag
* Dried beans or peas
* Water
* A bowl
* A notebook for your observations

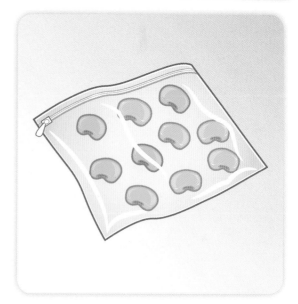

Can we use food waste to make energy?

Rotting waste can make a fuel people can use. How does this happen? Any **organic** material makes gas when it **decomposes**. Organic materials are made from plant or animal products.

Landfills of the future

What happens to the rubbish that you throw away? Most of our rubbish is buried in a **landfill**. At a landfill, there is little air and water, so organic waste rots very slowly. But some landfills are now being designed so that wastes will decompose more quickly. When organic wastes decompose, **methane** gas is produced. Methane is the same gas that is in **natural gas**. Landfill gas can be used as a fuel and to make electricity.

Landfill gas is carried in pipes from a landfill and is used to make electricity.

Methane is lighter than air, so it rises to the top of a landfill. Some landfills burn methane to get rid of it. But methane is a greenhouse gas and causes more global warming than carbon dioxide. Instead of burning it, some landfills now collect methane gas. Pipelines that are inside the landfill transport the gas. The gas can then be sold as a fuel. It can be burned to make steam and electricity.

Energy and you

Every day we use **energy**. Energy lights our homes and powers the machines we use. It keeps us warm in the winter and cool in the summer. We use energy to travel from home to school. Will there be enough energy for the future? That depends on the choices we make today.

Most of the energy we use today comes from **fossil fuels** that cannot be replaced. If we **conserve** energy, these **non-renewable resources** will last longer into the future. By using fewer fossil fuels, we create less air pollution and fewer gases that warm the Earth.

When you ride a bike instead of asking for a lift in a car, you save energy.

Saving energy

What can you do to conserve energy? You can ride a bike, take a bus, or walk to a friend's home. Share rides with friends and neighbours when you need to go by car.

Think of the many ways you can save energy in your home. Turn off lights, televisions, and computers when you are not using them. Teach others about what you have learned about saving energy. Start an energy conservation club at school.

We must all conserve energy to help take care of our planet.

Energy and the Earth

Our energy use has an impact on the air we breathe and on the planet. As people grow concerned about global warming, more **energy efficient** technologies are being developed. **Renewable energy resources** such as **solar energy** and wind energy may one day provide clean **electricity** for most people.

The future of the Earth and our energy resources depend on all of us. We must all conserve energy now. When you are an adult, you may have the choice of using new energy-efficient technologies that do not exist today. You might be the person who discovers a new source of energy that helps people in the future.

Glossary

alga (plural: **algae**) aquatic organism that uses the Sun's energy to make food. The remains of algae can form fossil fuels.

anemometer gauge for measuring the speed of wind

atmosphere gases surrounding Earth. Burning fuels can add gases to the atmosphere.

biodiesel fuel made from vegetable oils and animal fat, for use in a diesel engine. Biodiesel fuel can be made from waste oil from restaurants or from plants such as soybeans and rapeseed.

biomass plant material or animal waste that can be used as a fuel. Wood scraps from a timber company are burned to make steam and electricity.

carbon dioxide gas that is given off when fuels are burned and when living organisms break down food. Plants use carbon dioxide from the air when they make food.

compact fluorescent light bulb (CFL) Also known as energy-efficient bulbs. Compact fluorescent bulbs use less energy and last longer than incandescent light bulbs.

conserve use wisely. When we conserve resources, we are careful not to waste them.

decompose break down. The gas produced when material decomposes in a landfill can be used as fuel.

diatom single-celled alga that floats in the water. Diatoms that lived long ago are thought to be the source of oil.

electricity energy made available by the flow of an electric current. Wind power can make electricity.

energy source of power. Fossil fuel electricity and solar power are different kinds of energy.

energy-efficiency amount of useful work a machine gets from fuel. A car with high energy-efficiency uses less fuel.

ethanol fuel made from fermented plants. Ethanol is often mixed with petrol.

extinct no longer in existence. Climate change may cause some plants and animals to become extinct.

extract remove, especially by force

ferment chemical process in which sugars break down and alcohol is formed. Corn can be fermented to make ethanol.

fertilizer substance added to soil to help plants grow

fossil hardened remains of a plant or animal preserved inside rock

fossil fuel fuel that forms in the Earth from the remains of fossilized plants and animals. Oil, coal, and natural gas are fossil fuels.

generator machine that changes mechanical energy into electricity

global warming increase in the average temperature of the surface of the Earth

greenhouse effect process where the Earth's atmosphere traps the Sun's heat due to the presence of gases such as carbon dioxide, methane, and water vapour

hydroelectric generating electricity from the energy of running water. Hydroelectric power plants often have a dam that holds a reservoir of water.

incandescent light bulb bulb in which a filament is heated by an electric current. Incandescent light bulbs are less energy-efficient than compact fluorescent bulbs

insulation material that traps air. Insulation in the roof and walls of a home keeps heat inside during the winter.

kinetic energy energy possessed by a body in motion. Falling water has kinetic energy.

landfill large, outdoor area for rubbish disposal. The gas from a landfill can be used to make electricity.

methane gas that can be burned and used as a fuel

natural gas fuel that exists as a gas and can be burned for heat, cooking, and to make electricity

non-renewable resource natural resource that cannot be remade as fast as it is used. Fossil fuels are non-renewable resources.

organic material made from animal or plant compounds. Organic waste gives off gases when it rots.

peat spongy mass formed when plant matter is compressed. Peat can be burned as a fuel or used as a fertilizer.

photovoltaic cell device that converts the energy from sunlight into electricity. An array of photovoltaic cells mounted on a roof can produce electricity for a building.

pollutant unwanted substance that harms the environment, such as, sewage

potential energy energy in a body due to its position. Water held by a dam has potential energy.

recycle take unwanted material and make something useful out of it

renewable energy resource natural resource that can be replaced. Wind and solar energy are renewable energy resources.

reservoir lake used to store water for drinking. A reservoir can also be used to generate electricity.

smelt melt and separate a metal. Coal is used to smelt copper.

solar energy energy transmitted from the Sun. Solar energy can be used to heat water for a home.

turbine machine that is driven by the movement of water, wind, or steam. When a turbine that is connected to a generator spins, electricity is made.

Find out more

Books

A Bright Idea: Conserving Energy, Tristan Boyer Binns
   (Heinemann Library, 2005)

   This books answers questions about energy and explores ways you can
   conserve energy.

Earth's Precious Resources: Fossil Fuels, Ian Graham
   (Heinemann Library, 2004)

   This books shows how fossil fuels are found and processed.

Eco-Action: Energy of the Future, Angela Royston
   (Heinemann Library, 2008)

   This books looks at new technologies that will help reduce dependence on
   fossil fuels.

Renewable Energy, edited by Godfrey Boyle
   (Oxford University Press, 2004)

   This book looks at renewable energy sources including wind, solar, wave
   and geothermal energy.

Websites

Climate change
www.bbc.co.uk/climate/

See the evidence and impact of climate change and play the "I'm alright Jack" game.

Global warming maps
www.climatehotmap.org/

These maps show early warning signs of global warming in different countries.

Wave power
www.wavegen/com/

Watch a real-time webcam of a wave power device off the coast of Scotland.

Organizations

Energy Saving Trust
21 Dartmouth Street
London SW1H 9BP
0800 512012

www.energysaving trust.org.uk

This organization was set up by the government in the 1990's to help reduce UK emissions of carbon dioxide by 20 per cent by 2010.

Places to visit

Science Museum

Exhibition Road
London SW7 2DD
Tel: 0870 870 4868

www.sciencemuseum.org.uk/exhibitions/energy

The Science Museum has information and activities about different sources of energy.

Centre for Alternative Technology

Machyblleth
Powys, Wales
SY20 9AZ
01654 705950

www.cat.org.uk/

The Centre for Alternative Technology shows ways to work towards a sustainable future.

The Eden Project

Bodelva
St Austell
Cornwall, PL24 2SG
01726 811911

www.edenproject.com/

Index